A FEAST OF FOOLS

TERRY GIFFORD

INDEPENDENT INNOVATIVE INTERNATIONAL

Published by Cinnamon Press
Meirion House
Tanygrisiau
Blaenau Ffestiniog
Gwynedd, LL41 3SU
www.cinnamonpress.com

ISBN: 978-1-78864-008-4

British Library Cataloguing in Publication Data. A CIP record for this book can be obtained from the British Library.

Designed and typeset in Palatino by Cinnamon Press. Printed in Poland.

Cover design by Adam Craig from original artwork: leaping fools: 'The Fool' © Samiramay | Dreamstime

Cinnamon Press is represented in the UK by Inpress Ltd and in Wales by the Welsh Books Council.

Acknowledgements

Some of these poems have previously appeared in *Cadences, Poetry and Voice, Ecozon@, Interdisciplinary Studies in Literature and Environment, Environment and Organisation, Green Humanities, Green Letters, Critical Survey* and *Weber Studies*. 'Gemma' was first published in *Cat Kist: The Redbeck Anthology of Contemporary Cats*, edited by Jane Ramsden (Redbeck Press, 2004). 'Donkey' and 'The Bull of the Bernia' appeared in the anthology *Red Rock Dreaming* (McFarlands, 2014). 'In the Sorbonne' and 'Wordsworth Winter School' were included in *Teaching as a Human Experience* (Cambridge Scholars Press, 2015).

Quotation from Max Harris's *Sacred Folly: A New History of the Feast of Fools* used with kind permission of the author.
Quotation from Ted Hughes's 'Crow on the Beach' used with kind permission of Faber & Faber and the Ted Hughes Estate.

Contents

Flights of the Fool

El Bufón

The Guizer

'Christian biblical tradition acknowledges two kinds of fool. The first denies God's existence and authority [...] The second [...] is chosen by God because of his or her lack of worldly status [...] The Feast of Fools honoured the fool of lowly status.'

Max Harris, *Sacred Folly: A New History of the Feast of Fools*
(London: Cornell University Press, 2011: p.67).

His utmost gaping of brain in his tiny skull
Was just enough to wonder, about the sea,

What could be hurting so much?
Ted Hughes, 'Crow on the Beach', *Crow* (1970)

A Feast of Fools

In memory of tolerant roots
in Edna Gifford and Fred Gifford
and for the green shoots of
Islay, Elsbeth, Lewis, Rossi, Max, Amelie and Thea

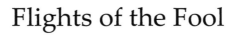

Flights of the Fool

Fatrasie

The poetic discourse used by the Fool in Medieval theatre.

If I am the fool, I address
an audience of fools,
my well-travelled fools,

my well-informed fools
making the journeys
of fools of our time.

Does the simplicity
of the harebell
confound you too?

Tell me what the blackbird
sings in his last song
clear as our air.

Did you miss his hand-
over to the owl who now
haunts your dreams?

Do hedgehogs out-
manoeuvre you too
on your lawns at night?

Do you fly, fools,
from what you do
not know in your land?

If I am the fool, I accept
an audience of fools,
my well-Googled fools,

my well-jetted fools
making the journeys
of fools of our time.

Watching Bald Eagles on my 59th Birthday

for Michael and Valerie Cohen

was present enough
    you'd think:
        leaving the cabin
earlyish, treading
    granite gravel
        high on hope,
the bird hunter
    a year older
        low on ambition
back sliding
    up the needle slope
        then firm on the friction
of the bald dome.
    Present enough
        the old eagle
on its white snag
    postage stamp still
        eye level
with eye and
    its treetop
        twig-tangle stirring.

Then greeting
    or warning
        or hunger,
it throws back
    its shaggy head
        beak open, emits
four needle stabs,
    spaced icy cries
        echoing over the lake.
Then, see, the lake
    is green now,
        not night blue,
in its glacial bowl,
    moraine boulder blocked,
        spotted with pines.

More reveals more:
        the redwing blackbird
                pings its three bells.
Above cars coming
        into the wooden town
                a woodpecker
plays its xylophone
        up the scale
                and human voices
share this birthday,
        rising from the still lake:
                families boat fishing.
Even the dead juniper
        mimes its many-armed
                death drama,
while lodgepole pines
        smoke their pollen
                on a new breeze.
So many gifts
        unwrapping each other
                before breakfast.

Talk of Apocalypse at Jamaica Pond

for Leo Marx

We stroll around your local pond
on the path Olmsted provided
for the purpose of taking in the light
and the cooler evening air
with conversation in this circle
of city calm, the jewel
of Olmsted's Boston necklace.
In his *sanitary institution*
water glints with wind,
bejewels a little space.

You break the swinging links
of conversation to say, *Listen.*
A Baltimore Oriole. A gem too dark
to see, but glistening in song above.
We talk of scientists' predictions
of apocalypse for new reasons.
Each has a shelf-life of a decade,
you observe, *before the pendulum*
of opinion swings back, countered.
That's a cardinal. We stop to attend.

Several pendulums seem high just now,
I suggest, as we are stopped again,
gazing at an island of two willows,
joined as one tree, holding high
black candles against the bright green
of low last light - cormorants
roosting improbably, evenly spaced,
as you've never seen them before,
(although your wife and daughter have,
each evening as you talk the walk).

The red lights of cars come on
across the pond where Olmsted's
broad carriageways now bring
commuters home. Since the sixties
your book has not been out of print:
The Machine in the Garden -
a necklace of roads, tracks, rockets
around the Eden of the earth.
To get home we need crossing lights
to halt those quietly fuming cars.

And the Bride Wore Trainers

for Doug Robinson

I .

In the early morning light we sit on the rimrock
and watch the Valley wake up fifteen hundred feet below,
the first cars crawling out of the trees past the meadow where
we brewed coffee in yesterday morning's steam of aromas.

That grand American Lodge, the Ahwahnee Hotel,
is a doll's house under our heels, an incongruous
stone structure dwarfed by the finest rock architecture,
these Royal Arches upon which we sit and read poetry

to each other in the still and somehow emotional air.
Grapefruit, bagels, bivi bags, coffee cups and pot,
were secreted in the packs on our backs climbing
Royal Arches yesterday in thirteen perfect pitches.

In the night two torch-less full-moon soloists rested, talking,
the other side of our bivi boulder. *Nothing but a boombox
between them,* you said. You had to press a bagel on them.
They even declined water, leaving for the notorious descent.
I heard only voices in the creek falling over the rim
in my jetlagged sleep. After filtered coffee from our
manzanita fire (the smallest twigs give most heat)
we each find poems in our packs, take them to the rim.

The next two days little is said, but much is given
and received, filtered, somehow, just by each other's
presence: nights on the ground, days in the open
(Jeffrey's pine needles make the best sleeping mat).

II

It doesn't matter that we don't climb North Dome.
Waiting, cloud watching, we see across the Valley
a green pollen cloud leave Glacier Point. *Those trees
are making love to this tree!* A Trickster's reaching
penis trick, I realise, like the up-thrust snow plant,
or the deep, low pumping sound of the grouse,
the very smell of the trail, the softness of everything
up here, the afterglow on snow peaks, second night:

No pencils were taken out.
Poets struck dumb at twilight.
Yosemite Point.
Gary Snyder's gift of form to us Americans, you say,
using it yourself here, like your manzanita tip, and
early morning of our final day, when you give me
the gift of moving over stone, knees bent between
walking and jogging, down the turning Yosemite Falls trail
to find a beer in the Ahwahnee Hotel, gatecrash a wedding,
watch the bride walk out into the meadow, stare upwards.

A Logjam on Lawson's Fork

for John Lane

Basketballs bob thick as frogspawn
against a snowline of polystyrene and plastic,
unmissed meltout from the upstream species,
filtered by last storm's fallen logs
above the bend where Cormac McCarthy's
brook trout still wimple softly,
their backs maps of the mystery
that cannot be made good again.

And this impaired piedmont creek drains
a suburban woodland lot in Spartanburg,
South Carolina, a hundred miles from wilderness,
although the deer step through still, the cold call
of the pileated woodpecker echoes through spring woods
lit by cardinals taking turns in the religious order
of their hierarchy at the birdfeeder and magical Mayapple
push through from toxic tubers in close-growing colonies
to swell a single apple under each green umbrella.

Here we walk and talk about your *Anthropocene*
Blues, pausing at the pawprint of a passing coyote,
your Anthropocene survivor, and hear
the chainsaw sound, cross-river, of your neighbouring
kid's quad bike phase that you'll outwait,
you say, learning from a larger sense of time.
When didn't where we live compromise
how we live? When didn't how we live
compromise where we are? When weren't we
being filtered by the logjam at Lawson's Fork?

The View from Dead Horse Point

is deeper, wider than our language.
Words do caption the postcards,
pale pictures inscribe the T-shirts.
But out here, in leathers, his helmet hidden,
the staring motor-cycle warrior
from Minnesota, our only shaman
at this early hour, is still in trance.
This is why he rides each year down
the continent to Dead Horse Point,
rises in darkness from his Moab motel
to encounter time and silence:
dawn at Dead Horse Point.

But he can't stay silent for long.
It has a quality, he says, *all other places
lack somehow.* For us it had been just
another road out of Moab towards another
bend in a river, another night in the car
(an electric storm over Canyonlands, all clothes
and handbrake on). At dawn this maze of bends
ignites in light so bright we too are sunk
in meditation until our traveller tells the tale
of his life-journey that brings him here.
We listen in wordless witness before
the view from Dead Horse Point.

Anazazi Canyon Culture

We all live together
under the basket of father sky
in the bowl of mother earth
with the spirits of all things.
Our job is to care for them.

From the basket we dropped
into the bowl of the Four Corners
riding the spirit of oil to hear
the Ranger quote the Navajo
in a roofless house for reading stars.

In a turnout on the rim road
now linking these ancient sites,
our hire-car is parked up
behind the shiny RVs and SUVs,
locked, with their engines running.

From a board we all read together how
the Anazazi alcove dwellers used
the yucca leaf for rope, snares,
sandals and paintbrushes, the root
for soap before sacred ceremonies.

Luciferin

tiny stars hang

               in the black curtains

                              either side of the track

in New

               Zealand

                              fern palm bush

night's little lights

               of Hine-nui-te-pō

                              female seductions

oxidising enzymes

               luciferin in the water

                              of invisible bodies

making pale lights

               blue/green

                              glowing in their silence

not of a worm

               but a beetle

                              Lampyris noctiluca

warm stillness

               the gift

                              of our guides

Alan

               and luci

                              ferin

Tapu, North Island, NZ

At the Great Dune you can see
the souls of the dead
always on the move
towards the northern Cape,
the place of leaping.
The glistening mica grains
bleached of life, but speaking
a surf spirit between breakers
and bush, move in their millions
down and across the dune veins,
a form agreed mysteriously,
precisely, uniformly,
by gravity and wind.
Mile-wide and mountainous
at the Great Dune,
these Maori souls creep

up North Island's *tail of the fish*
to the sea-flick of Cape Reigna
for the final leap of departure
from a *Tapu* signed tourist place.
And through the flat break
of the braiding Te Paki Stream
the 90 Mile Beach buses
splash landwards at low tide
on their daily ecotourism trip
between ocean and dunes,
whale-water and soul-sand,
pausing only for boogie-boarding
(*Hire boards from the caravan*)
the majestic Great Dune.

Mansions in the Mountains of Paradise

are hidden behind trees
feathering darkly from ravines:
wet falls of paper
streaked with moss
and a smudged mist.

In a low rafia of roots
is the frail bridge
that brings a path
back up the scroll
through inky trees

to what is hardly
a human habitation.
This is our mansion
in the humid hills
of paradise,

said Tang Yuan
to his wife searching
scroll after scroll
for the right inscription
to give to his work.

18th October in the Old Calendar

for Chen Hong

Driving back to Wuhan last
November down the new highway,
straight as a government decree,
the evening mists gathered
about the banked rice ponds
at the passing roadsides.
The water buffalos had disappeared
into new sheds that now were home.
It was more grey than dark.

Suddenly the fireworks started,
first a single star-shower of
red, white and green falling into
a vague cluster of rooftops.
Then another, and another, rising
behind the last, lifting and falling
back, rushing up and reaching out,
bud-bursting and leaf-drifting down
into unseen upturned faces

warming to the wedding tomorrow,
a Saturday, after harvest, an eight
in the date of the old calendar,
eighteenth of October best of all,
never mind that it's November
in the warming world of solar panels,
Western white-wedding photographs,
in these state villages of new houses.
Right and left of us rockets lit the sky.

The Wounded Kite

was bought by the wide river in Wuhan
one kite-flying Sunday when each romantic couple
had one tied to a finger as they walked the esplanade.
On a Scottish holiday that kite hung to the left, wanted
to die in a beach dive again and again—granddad
losing credibility again against the perfect sand
where dad handled a huge kite that needed a harness
and wheeled board to cruise the empty strand.

That beautiful kite, granddad's gift from the heart of China
where a kite-filled sky was anchored by smiling citizens
flying mythical beasts, all steady in their stable state,
that kite, lovely as it looked, was the product of an unbalanced
economy: capitalist socialism had somehow failed to be equal
with the glue on the left wing and the right wing
so that gravity brought it down with a stunning impact.

Granddad, the old diehard, kept trying again and again
with undiminished enthusiasm to lift the spirits of the air,
of kite-flying China, of his young family who, of another era,
sat back in the sand and simply laughed and laughed.

In the Sorbonne

we discuss
>the quality
>>of yellow light

in the painting
>and in the poem
>>about the painting.

The grey heads
>shake at the
>>impossibility

of *yellow light.*
>The students smile
>>at memories

of yellow light
>through curtains
>>on delicate hair.

Beyond
>the delicious
>>discourse of the room,

framed
>by high windows
>>of history,

the pale light
>on soft stone
>>is impossible

as yet
>to be named
>>*yellow.*

Wassa Museum, Stockholm

It stood no chance, that was obvious
to any observer of the disproportions:

the thin waist and the corpulent superstructure,
the slim-keeled innocence, the lack of ballast

and the voluble complexity of knowledge
carved in detail from Roman and pagan myths.

Doomed to sink before its life began,
launched into deep waters, downwards,

silted over and forgotten for 400 years,
ages eclipsing such stunning possibility,

such a frisson of full-sailed promise,
such sincerity crafted in every timber

with every touch of the chisel, every smile
at the making of the beautiful impossibility:

the difference between a bicycle and a cab
by which they arrived, the youthful student

and the aging professor who actually avoided
the need for a fumbling futility of explanations

for years to come, the embarrassing enquiry,
with the king still away, fighting in Poland.

Antarctica

You know the way a sparrowhawk
will slip away from a winter wood,
ease free of those bronze bones
into the field of fired last light
before you'd noticed it was there—

you know the way the full moon
crept, crepuscular, from behind
that hill somehow, silent, so close
someone should have shouted out
as you do now at a moment missed—

or the way you can watch the sun
being eaten by our earth's wide lip,
but you can never see it rise,
lift its eyelid, even in the Outback
you blink and it's already happened—

that's how they drifted apart
over the years, water passing,
incremental cooling, volcanoes
declared dormant, sap slowed
to a calcite fossil at the core.

El Bufón

The Storks of Alcalá

In the street café before the conference
I treated myself to exquisite notes in
my new Moleskine notebook, smallest size,
with my favourite Berol Fine felt-tip pen
about the storks of Alcalá performing
above the square flying banners boasting
Five hundred years of welcoming students.

Above the bells, I wrote, *like small green
castanets in their towers, the huge nests add
something older to the Medieval architecture,
something of wood woven over thousands of years.
Down their long beaks the storks now look upon
the new colours of cars, and the university dons
in gold-edged gowns of the fifteenth century.*

*Kiting with a low loop into the street
a stork with orange legs flies ...* into
a wine blot and out ... *so many centuries before.*
Later, in the gilded hall of the university,
rampant with heraldry of lions, and storks,
the gowns process to their high seats. The Director
asks the Mayor, who asks his wife, for a pen.

Donkey

What Valencian counting rhymes
were chanted between the narrow walls
of Pas de Comptador, allowing one goat
at a time and always a funnelled wind?

These days we can breach it in our little 4x4,
the sun already set behind Cabeçó d'Or
and on the old road name, Camí Real.
We looked down the length of the Barranc de l'Arc

towards home, a return to the womb, rich
with shadows among olives and almond trees,
and the white veins of tracks and trails
we knew so well from years of walking here.

But we did not know of a single donkey
left in the Barranc de l'Arc and here was one
standing still and ghostly pale at the foot
of the steep rutted slope from the pass.

Its long trailing rope told the story.
It was reluctant to get quite so close
to the tree to which we tied it,
using all the rope in a donkey-proof knot.

Questions, questions, as we drove on down
the long valley floor until we saw a man:
leather jacket, scarred brown face, wild hair.
Did he know anyone who kept a donkey?

That donkey, he said without a smile, *eats*
and eats all day getting fatter and fatter.
So each evening I take her for a walk.
I was wondering where she was.

Well, we tied her to a tree back there.
We thought she had escaped. Sorry.
He was gracious, this hermit from
the highest house in the valley.

Thank you, he said, turning back.
What Valencian curses carried on the wind
that night? And in the talk at the next market,
how many donkeys were in this story?

Fira de Mostres i Cultura Mediterrània, Sella, 2013

Tables and houses open to the heat and the visitors,
Plaza Major decked like a Moorish ship under sail
displaying its pirated goods and treasures usually
locked in the caskets of memory, family tradition
and the long years of hands and feet crafting cooking
and dances and music and designs and techniques for
growing well with garlic and oil and an unspoken love.

Here's the doctor, smoking, bold with fiery hair beside
the priest whose interests are food and fun and people
next to the beautiful president of fiestas accompanying
the mayoress, youngest in all of Spain, smiling, smiling
alongside the tattooed Englishman semi-resident, semi-sane.
Here's a line of judges spooning and chewing and nodding
approval of food fresh from the dark alchemy of kitchens.

Here is a house displaying the recent story of the village
that Pepe el Llop remembers: the first bridge, the first
electricity, the first public water pumps and telephone,
the first school library. And the old ladies who carry the story,
the hard memories, the smiles of remembered reputations of
the personalities—every figure in a photo a known name—
talk the history in the vernacular of this proud special place.

And here at the end of Calle Angel the musicians gather,
not at all nervous, tuning and toasting a dram to Aurora, smiling
and joking at the arriving friends, each falling into their role
of the loud guitar, the slightly out of tune mandolin,
the enthusiastic singer of a song that welcomes the dawn
with the single (new) drum of the plumber, the street-wandering
rhythm that calls the village into living its pagan-religious life.

And here are the skipping dancers upon delicately strung feet
turning like sails in a gentle wind fingering the street breeze,
white pinafores presenting a virgin front, wide tumbling skirts
hiding a great volume of secrets from their mothers (and others).
Giggles reveal the mistakes that go unnoticed by the doting crowd
as whispers unravel kindly among the breathless, just finished,
until again the Moorish singing calls them into line to ebb and to flow.

And here's the poet pulled in to judge the eight dishes
of alioli (although he'd rather judge wine) just made
with that special twist of the wrist on the pestle in mortar
and at the last moment an addition of salt and something secret,
but a draw is declared and the eager crowd decide that Maria
has won with a creamy unsalty concoction that delivers
a kick like a mule. And so, on, with no time to mention

the pilota, the ballad singer Botifarra whose eye-widening tales
bring tears of laughter, the school of pilota, the crowded launch
of Mila's Sella-set novel sold out in seconds, the exhibition
of the history of village pilota, traditional techniques for trapping
birds, the book of the history of village pilota, and on, to Isabel
La Roja's demonstration of how all this was always woven
together in Sella by the grounded green strength of esparto grass.

That Orange Tree

is hidden like a jewel
in a box of jewels.
Reach, pull, pluck, peel,
taste, until you find it
in the far corner, but
not exactly the corner
of the orange grove
we amble through
under the Moorish castle.

Like eating chocolate,
said my father, *and no mistake.*
In every orange grove
there is a bitter tree
that is bypassed
when the baskets are dragged.
But every tree is different:
early, late, easy, awkward, best.

That orange tree the neighbours
know and wait while the pruning,
ploughing, banking, flooding,
bring blossom to fruit
and fruit to fullness
to plunder under a new year's moon.
Kant died from eating too many
Cheddar sandwiches, we're told —
a serious empirical error.

The Bull of the Bernia

I think it was my curiosity that caused it
and perhaps you were right that it had
put us both in danger high on the open
mountainside amongst the Bernia's bulls
where a simple afternoon of walking the track,
grazing bulls below us, suddenly turned violent.
Was it because I stopped? Was it because I wondered
what that young bull saw behind my eyes
from its still, staring, glassy eyes locked on mine
that it answered my question with an explosion
of legs, muscle, horns that carried a hurt of the heart
into my outstretched walking poles in its head.

Into my outstretched walking poles in its head
legs, muscles, horns that carried a hurt of the heart,
that answered my question with an explosion
from its still, staring, glassy eyes locked on mine
was what that young bull saw behind my eyes.
Was it because I stopped? Was it because I wondered
grazing bulls below us suddenly turned violent
where a simple afternoon of walking the track
on the mountainside amongst the Bernia's bulls
put us both in danger, high and open?
And perhaps you were right that it had.
I think it was my curiosity that caused it.

(Eagle, sunset)

and just below the summit
going the wrong way
back down the ridge
to find the descent gap
you thought you remembered
that we hadn't looked down,

rock slightly slippery
under sharp bushes,
the cold wind of night
sprung from somewhere,
the chill certainty, now
of benightment before
reaching the track to the car.

No time to notice
the eagle, its slow drift
on big wings above us,
as I check that the sun
is definitely down
behind the black horizon
that moments before

was a bank of shafted
shadows you'd found time
to photograph. Now
we must stay together,
backs to the summit
I know we must return to.
It hurts to lose this height
and light, but you are calm

and say this gap must
at least be eliminated
and should have been
when first we crossed
in haste below the crest.
We look down at
an undescendable drop,
sheer and all wrong.
We turn again

towards the summit.
Now the way is clear
to cross its crest
and find the gap
that leads to the rock
scramble you found
last trip up here. A ramp,
then route-finding
downwards to darkness.
It must be done.

Walking Early from Relleu

for Gill

It is of such sweat that love poems are made.
Frederico García Lorca

Pure white above the before dawn
yellow of the nun's long legs, but stained,
as with sweat from a long night's travel
across cloudless sky, now promising
the faintest hint of pink along her profile,
the moon drops, with almost motionless grace,
its pretence to know day, this strengthening orange
blood on the face of the still sleeping nun.

There is no guilt in her going,
her so subtle self-eclipse,
no self-harm in her cutting the hill
so slowly. No scent of her sweat remains,
only moon memory marking the choices
to be made in the bright light of day
creeping towards us down the habit
of our own footfalls and hard sweat.

Segóbriga

Here, like a Tuscan hill town, walled
on the steepest rise in La Mancha,
its sheer side the rocky river bluff,
Rome carved its grid into Spain.

      Now it faces black fields of upturned
      tilted tables, a grid of solar panels
      like vast banks of bees' honeycomb
      melting energy as they soak up the sun.

Wood fuelled, Caio Iulio Silvano's house
kept a shrine to Zeus carved in Greek, warmed
by oak and birch cut for fields of corn.
Below, the watermill turned for *tostados*.

      Lined along the horizon now,
      like a knoll of grand old oaks,
      white turbines turn in La Mancha wind
      slowly saying, *Y? Y? Y?*

Lapis specularis the Romans mined here,
the new technology's window glass,
and spring water ran in stone conduits
siphoned over hills for five kilometres.

      The new motorway winds below,
      sucking the last oil from the earth,
      past rolling ranks of sad sunflowers,
      dead heads hung for future fuel.

A whisper on the platform of the theatre
still carries to the gods, and stalls for wild
beasts still stink under the amphitheatre
where five thousand sat, as for a bullfight

      in the civilised city of modern Madrid.

Among Vultures, Alcoi

From a natural rock bench
we sit and peer over the rim
of the plunging ravine among
the cruising Pterosaurs
passing above, below — slow
as the sun burning our backs.

From a black eye aligned with the beak
through the white head we're flicked
a glance of utter disdain
straight from the Late Jurassic
where the wind's constancy
widened these barn-door wings,
their black-shadowed trailing edge
circling the scents of death on
rising thermals from barren earth.

Entranced, we watch for hours
as evolution unravels before our eyes.
Two birds now wear gold
wing-tags like jewellery, fluttering
their individuality audibly
as they pass. Now they have
numbers from a species counting
its years. But the birds already
have trained the butchers
from the noisy town below
to leave carrion on the plateau.
This is also a new development,
like the evolution of the town
by a species exchanging gold. It will go.
For this is the landscape of vultures.

The Door of Mari Chaves

How powerful is your own front door
as your self-declaration to the street?
In Murcia, the door of Mari Chaves
so shocked and frightened the Inquisition
that they preserved it in their chamber of horrors
to now become an art-work of civic pride:
twenty carved icons are inset in two doors —
phantasms of astrology, bestiality, cabala —
of the Portuguese seer, healer, sage.

What dangerous depths were conjured
by those more-than-three-dimensional
horrors: the comb-ribs of a sitting horse
with a human face; the bull's head of a green
man; two lions in standing embrace;
the griffon; the jester; the long-bearded man
with clawed feet; the curled creature of tails,
trails of thin wings; the winged goat of wisdom;
the Cancer crab of the stars, the stars.

What writhing thing is that human holding?
How does his hand curl round his back?
On the left is crouching Pan, penis erect;
on the right door, crouching wide open,
hands gripping long hair, is Sheila-na-gig.
Satyr, centaur, basilisk, dragon, moon-face,
leonine mask and green man are hybrids
of healing animal helpers, or monstrous
mutants of devilish powers in our heads.

Here in the cool silence of Murcia's museum
among paintings of religious suffering
and joyous peasant harvesting, is displayed
a door seized by Christians in seventeen-twenty,
La Puerta de Mari Chaves — fortune teller,
herb-healer, mixer of medicines in
alchemy, magic, cosmic compassion —
the Jewish sorceress from abroad who, after
a second trial, was burned alive as a witch.

Three Peaks
Into the Future:
Water, Fire, Rockfall

Walking far too fast
from Finestrat's Font Moli,
tripping over tree roots
in a dark start again
until, in a chill
gunmetal grey light,
we surprise the hunter,
a peregrine echoing
high on Puig Campana.
Rounding its summit track
we look down and back
on Benidorm's towers
sucking the ground water
from under our feet.

Descending to the Col de Pouet
we push on towards Ponoch
but take five in a bower
to be burned in the fire
begun in Polop next weekend
when we watch from Sella
a red horizon leaping.
On the summit, in cycle shorts,
stands our village chemist,
deaf and dumb, an able
reader of lips, who leaves
to look over the rim
at what will become black
tree-bones and ash.

Sanchet is all rock,
and heavy in our heads
on the horizontal donkey
trail below its looming
spine. A siesta is essential
and an orange, a fresh
stance: *poc a poc*, boulder
by bolder steps to find
on this summit the Hut
Bookings Secretary from
my climbing club, one eyebrow
plastered, I notice, as we pass
below a scar of recent rockfall,
a stark future seen for miles.

The Hummingbird Hawkmoth

had kept me staring into the almond tree—
a chameleon among the blossom—
transfixed by the bobbing thimble
that could hang on a thread to needle
the pink heart of frail white petals.

So when the path led to the olive tree
in front of the highest house, its empty door,
in the deserted village, I understood
the stillness of the young man outside
in the long grass staring into the tree, head

slightly askew, intent on something
up there and I approached silently, noticed
his white nose-and-mouth-mask that, closer,
became a rope attached to a branch and
at his feet a chair on its back in the grass.

Winter Wood Smoke

The evening wood smoke wafts across the village roofs,
warm and already redder than ever in cosy houses
with the blood of the ancient olive trees, prudently pruned.
The sun has sailed from Campana to a fold in Aguilar
where the mottled trees absorb its winter secret gift.
Soon the Campana will ring with red and the Peña de Sella
light up its movie screen of shifting colour above us all.

Yesterday we buried Antonio, the kindest, most generous
man of the village whose numbers gave access to the doctor
and whose old Mercedes took villagers to the hospital,
quietly going about his business, in the Sella way.
He drew a car park full of cars to his own final journey.
In the huerta he loved, he finally fell, far too soon,
too much now lost of the old village values we must revive.

But more has changed, as the water to the huerta has thinned —
the wine crop has failed and almonds hang dried up in their shells.
Mushrooms eluded searchers like pious monks, heads down,
quartering the October fields of the dark side of Aitana.
This year's olive oil is missing, having skipped a crop,
although these family friends have outlasted almond trees
that are dying on their feet from more than smoke of wood.

Solemn Procession in Honour of *la Divina Aurora*

This is the moment of stillness
at the pulsing heart of the fiesta.
This is the moment when something
is passed from the old to the young
who may not even be here, asleep, beating
to a different drum. The drum, the drum
hushes the gossip, the blood of the village,
as the Plaza Major falls expectant, heavy
church bells tolling, two reeds and the drum,
the drum: black, slow, passing, three-
part music from the Medieval village,
the ancient Sella, prickling hairs now,
alive in the presence of the high cross,
before two lines of dripping candles,
the fire of life remembering the dead,
walk past as we stand in respect, knowing
their black and their white, old and young,
stories and dreams, knowing and unknowing,
all processing under the big church bell,
the fiesta blue lights, the streamers, the church
door open to all, sucking all into its arms
as the *majorales* in the costumes of tradition
sway left, sway right, as though with the weight
of Aurora in their steps, striped socks
and waistcoats, before the Virgin, heavy
with flowers, candles and climate change—
the new dawn of desertification, the few
heavy terrace-tumbling rains—processing
to its drum under this apparent stillness.

Casc Antic

What is hiding here?
    Which many-headed Minotaur
        just turned these corners of history?

The blind man knows
    whose fingers read these walls
        hearing the cries, the sighs, the bullets.

Whose stone speaks here?
    What many-voiced lord
        squeezed sweat from these hills?

The street women know
    whose whispers draw from wells
        the blood with the water.

Whose freedom is this?
    What many-legged passions
        have run through these streets?

These chipped corners know
    giving and taking
        what was never still, never theirs.

What are these smells?
    What many-waved seas
        wash through these walled vents?

The city sharks know
    and their tanned victims
        turning under a terrible sun.

What will empty the old town?
    What many-decades-long tentacles
        will suck people to the slim river?

The old seer knows
    staring through unfinished apartments
        watching for rain, and the slowly rising sea.

The Guizer

Mobiles

It was a preference for the Quiet Coach -
Wait at the last blue bench along
the platform, sir—that produced, full frontal,
the Didcot Cooling Towers, famous
architect designed *Cathedral of the Vale*,
and circling on hidden strings above
the town, distant Red Kites, flapping.

Six dark angels in a reddening sky
mirrored the inverted shapes of six
still towers settling into the past
from which these Kites are revived
to scavenge our civilisation, this station
where all heads are pulled down over
little lit digital screens, flickering.

Watching the Year in Derbyshire

The Swift month
starts the year
scouring cartwheels
through the sky.

The Martin month
needs mud and
hospitality, moving chairs
away from walls.

In the Plover month
the moors emit
a plaintive cry calling in
the cruising Harrier.

It is considered lucky
in the Merlin month
to glimpse a pulse
of arrow over heather.

Waiting by water,
watching a dead snag,
the Osprey month
makes its own luck.

Chattering telephone wires,
taut with nervous
fears of flying, speak of
the gathering Swallows month.

After the first frost,
before the full fogs,
you will know if you have
missed the Wryneck month.

So will there be
this year, before
or during snow,
a Snow Bunting month?

More reliable
at Beeley Triangle -
the low kite-skimming
of Short-Eared Owl month.

Quiet on black fingers,
here already, a fist of sticks
under the overhang —
Raven nesting month.

Returning to the belfry
in the heart of the city -
the stooping moustache
of Peregrine month.

Among gritstone boulders,
not far from water, still
homing in to its old hole,
Ring Ouzle month returns.

Snowdrops at Fairy Cave Quarry

The bank is a breathtaker
of snow after the snow
above the quarrymen's wall,
under rewilding woods
of young ash and pale birch.

It is a bank of stars
somehow thrusting through
spoil on this slope
from an evolutionary drive
to repossess one corner

for flying a white flag
against the dulling of winter:
black leaf mould,
lichened wet stone,
the cold drips of trees.

But here something is singing
an unlikely song of sheer joy:
Galanthus nivalis galloping
away from James Allen's
grasp for Magnet and Merlin,

the urban monocots of
Shepton Mallet. Here, hidden
like caves, perennial petaloids
swell and spring forth as
the very song of Spring.

Spring Lyric

You know the way that music starts
beyond your bedroom window, urgent,
instant, and it's dark. What time is it?

Blackbird singing through the dead of night …
To this bird it was not night and
there were no dead. On the contrary.

Last night I listened, as Vaughn Williams had,
for *The Lark Ascending*, not notating nature
in my case, but being led by the melodic line.

Finally, I turned, pulled the pillow deeper,
knew my need for sleep as working lyric poet
with tutorials each ten minutes in the morning.

But it was no good. Take advantage? Drive to the hide
at Redmires Reservoir to seek the short-eared owl
ghosting about with sudden turns into the heather?

Last year I was prey to this pre-dawn addiction.
Last night I wasn't. I read and returned to sleep.
At work, two storks have settled on the chimneys.

They've overshot the north of France.
For six hundred years here no-one's heard their cry
which I now call *complaint*, thinking I know

about the lyric, night and day, each end
of the commute across the seasons
as I try to sleep and work, teach and write.

Slug

A slug came to my wine cup
on a dark, wet evening,
and I in shorts for the summer
and a fleece.

Under the deep, thick shade of the privet hedge
I came up the steps to my tent
from deep in the bowels of the valley
and the great wet trees smoking
silently.

Someone was before me at my mug
scenting its rich Sicilian wine,
poised at its rim, softly,
his slack black body
trailed down the far side
as I lifted the cup to drink
and met one of the lords of life
looking around like a god, unseeing,
on my plastic wine mug,
snake-easing his shoulders
in the night air.

A sort of horror, a sort of protest
at his horrid slow speed,
that he had come like a guest in quiet, to drink at my wine cup
made me look round, pick up a clumsy plate
and prise him off the white plastic
and I thought of the albatross
and I thought of the wine
from the hot slopes of Etna smoking.

And I drank
from my side of the mug
having something to expiate,
a pettiness.
and in the wet grass of morning
that underworld was writhing
slowly
with small, pale new slugs.

I had missed my chance,
in the wine-deep sleep of July
to hear the Osiris-cry of
slug shout.

My Father Met Ted Hughes

He was on his knees pulling weeds
in the Fellows Garden, now on a kneepad,
but trilby, jacket, tie: on duty Head Gardener.

Ted had wanted to meet him before
the reading at Kings, retiring into green
shade with the shyness of a fisherman.

As we passed through the sacred gate,
still forbidden to the young, an aged don,
greeting my father, received a touch of Dad's hat.

Isn't this the lawn of 'Thrushes'? I said.
No, the Library, Ted replied, ever terse. *And the pond
of 'Pike'?* I ventured. *That I never tell.*

Even at this distance, my father's hands
were lumpish roots of earth-cunning, his face
a fresh swede from the Fens, offering help.

Ted took his measure as Dad arose stiffly,
waited, momentarily, for my father to straighten,
and held out his own huge unworn hand.

The Poet Laureate wanted to meet you, Dad,
I began, but fell silent. Eye to respectful eye,
two green men were speaking to each other.

Two Hander

i.m. Jim Curran

After father's music and mother's milk
the left hand sucks a pencil,
the right hand bites the bug
of rounded rock at Harrison's
and neither knows quite
what the other's doing
out there, obsessively,
in the wild explorations
of their elemental extremities,
laughing, loving, drinking
it all in for much, much, later.

After the rock, the snow,
after the photos, the films,
after the films, the books,
after the books, the speaking
of the one hand to the other
from pencil portraits of comrades
and casualties, to remembered
mountains—stark, hard playgrounds
of light and driven mists—
and monumental crags, hidden
in the fabled woods like Harrison's.

Pachyderm

An elephant's elegant eyelashes form
a fine brush, an uneven black curtain
through which to view the world
with a watery eye of almost disdain,
remembering what it was like before
people came in their cars of all colours,
wobbled out on white thin legs,
came patting, fast-talking, looking,
looking and leaving for the lions.

And the elephant, too, is always moving
its three-fingered trunk about the ground,
or periscope sniffing the air for what's
on the wind—forewarned—not complacent,
but both strong and delicate, touching
and smelling both high and low with ripples
of rubber skin that is both rough and soft.

Its trunk is already packed for all journeys,
for whatever may be required: feeding
the tongue, grooving back grass seeds,
or manoeuvring branches for breaking
on its rack of yellow back teeth, sucking
or blowing for drinking or washing,
whatever is called for as the cars rust.

And the elephant is always slowly moving
in its different timescale, far-seeing a different
outcome, knowing, somehow, the most reliable
water-holes in the thin, ash-dusted forests,
the long grasses of broken-fenced plains,
in the rough and soft folds of the hills
that always were pachyderm skin—all
elephantine free-range homeland again
as in the empty cities the cars slowly rust.

Gemma

She was ready to die, knew it was time,
stopped lapping at water held out before her.

>On lawns, lakes and low ground, white
>winter mist cuts off trees at the roots.

Sixteen years ago she followed a divorce:
Mum, now we can keep a cat!

>Shrunk back into branches, still stems,
>the patience of trees diminishes us.

Whiskers a mile wide, she'd kept to the garden,
failed to catch bird, mouse or butterfly.

>In boles and holes, under branches,
>white pupae keep the small birds alive.

Children fledged, mother abroad, she crept
into her box in back of the garage to die.

>Night comes fingering through the fog
>and the fox unfurls for her dustbin patrol.

The weight of night's ice prunes the woods.
The death of our cat diminishes us.

Wordsworth Winter School

The deer in the mist
    out in the meadow
        early morning

beyond the bend
    in the fast-running
        February brook

looked up at us
    disappointed
        but unsurprised

as, on our side, we were
    also surprised but
        somehow rewarded

for our before-breakfast
    unpromising
        walk in the drizzle

to disturb local deer
    withdrawing now to woods
        as we withdrew

to discuss in our groups
    whether deer in mist
        can make a poem

in themselves
    for Wordsworthian
        post-pastoralists

or whether such a poem
    needs the knowledge,
        for example,

that this very spot
    in time may be
        the Ambleside bypass.

Cairngorm

Rising above the last hump
of wild hill, blown brown,
wind-trammelled and wet,
the snows of Ben Macdui
lie back between the black
knuckles of the mountain's fist,
clenched against a sky tearing
across the Cairngorms' fragile skin,
worn now as much by walkers
as by winters, their technical boots
kicking at bare bones.

And is the naked stone of this fist,
the sub-arctic jewel of Scotland,
clenched against the National Park,
or gleaming in the centre of its ring?
Cairngorm—a chairlift, a restaurant, now
a funicular. The ptarmigan croaks
still in the corries crossed by eagles, but
how could the snow bunting have halted
that funicular in appeals to EU law?

Crystal Ridge—glinting hand-grazer,
crumbling its crystals under climbers' feet
and Cairngorm thaws, poised between
rock, snow and run-off to the sandy glen.
It speaks only of isolation and change:
Wilderness Permits, Bike Bans,
Radio-linked Rangers, less snow,
more zoning, campaigns to save the midge.

The Wearing of the Motley:
The Cioch Nose of Sgurr a' Chaorachain

Did it begin with that huge Hooded Crow
at the campsite as we pulled out early morning
standing on the windscreen wiper of the yellow truck
puzzled by that other Hooded Crow mocking him?

Or did it begin the night before the long drive
at the Bristol Tobacco Factory's Forest of Arden
with *books in the running brooks, / Sermons in stones*
and a girl dressed as a boy pretending to be herself?

Or the improbable descent path, as of a sea cliff?
Or the mocking first move of a *Classic Rock* V. Diff,
off-balance off width, expanded fist-jam or long, long reach,
more free from peril than the envious court?

Then *consecutive tricky corners*, seduced by a stuck Friend,
became a tricky traverse into the correct corner left of a roof.
More mocking was the thrutchy corner requiring a knee
and sack-hauling, a finger-lock and forced momentum.

Tom sat on *one of the best belay ledges in Scotland,*
after weeks of weather forecast watching: a dry Saturday,
high cloud, out of that churlish chiding of the winter wind,
son and old father in exile, the only fools in the deer forest.

All that looked chunky from below steepened to high steps.
The exposed wall of thin footholds revealed incuts and a peg.
Another puzzling Hard Severe move had a Moac at hand level.
All chimneys were grooves and all lay-backs short-lived.

Finally, all summits were false, the first a formidable
wall of rock-steps threaded by a path and a pitch.
Now came the six necks to down-climb that no-one mentioned.
But climbers like it necky, and the wearing of the motley.

Hinkley G

Blinding morning sunlight
    reflects from rippled sand
        still running with rivulets
            of star-pulled tide-drain,
                the old energy, undated
                    as yet,
                        for decommissioning.

St Davids' Misericords

I

Matins, Lauds, Prime—the elderly priests stood
for the day's divine offices—Terce, Sext, None,
plus the Mass, collapsing at Vespers and Compline.

Even the mercy of seats in the choir stalls
was mitigated by goose-hinging them upwards
leaving a little shelf to soften the misery of standing.

The Medieval seat carvers knew that, Janus-like,
their seats faced both ways: whilst Latin psalms
rose up here, the Green Man reigned below,

the fat dragon flew, serpents seethed, ears to the ground,
grapes in vines flourished, a boat needed repairing,
the master craftsman working whilst the apprentice drank.

Where the pigs can devour the wolf, the bishop
has the body of a goose and is tempted by the woman,
goose-headed, with much noise and little sense,

who offers the bread and wine to fox the goose
into unholy marriage. How she leans towards him
under the singing, Matins to Sext to Compline.

II

Inside the cathedral the boat rides
the heavy swell in the wooden carving
rising around its clinkers in cadences
that come with the wind of West Wales.

Outside the cathedral cliff-top campers
check their anchors against the swell
of hooped nylon tents like upturned boats:
prows against the weather of West Wales.

Inside the cathedral the boatman strains
back upon his steering oar to hold
the bow towards the wind whilst St Govan
is being sick into the sea of West Wales.

Outside the cathedral small white horses
toss wetsuited canoeists from their plastic shells
into the heavy cadences of gasping breaths
beside their boats in the water of West Wales.

Inside the cathedral St Govan's two companions
offer comfort, one laying a soft hand on his head,
the other, lying back against the bow, signs
a benediction on travellers from West Wales.

Outside the cathedral the dead dolphin
rides the heavy swell in a cleft of cliff,
an upturned boat in a nave of stone,
beyond benediction, but signing in West Wales.

MacDara's Day Regatta, 2016

for Robert Jocelyn

The silence spoken on the boat is Irish.
All stare ahead, focussed hard on forward
momentum, ignoring other hookers on a collision
course. 'This is your boat!' I'd suddenly been told,

rushed forward to scramble from launch to hooker:
Matt Casey's *Colmcille*. Old Matt put his face
in mine. 'What's your name?' Our only exchange.
This boat is a play by Samuel Beckett

in the Irish of South Connemara: a sea-road
and a tree, luff rigged. We are cruising for position.
A hooter, and now a scrambled hoisting of the jib.
I'm climbing uphill over Connemara kerbstones –

the boat's ballast in the bottom of the hold –
to brace against the breast-high gunnel, taste
this rising Atlantic by the bucketful and stay alert
for the killer boom, grasping a jib sheet peg.

What does it mean, this play of shaped wood
and cut canvas for reading wind and meeting wave
with art and silence and the finest trim of the fleet
to steer through the open throat of the ocean

and roll up and over its unrelenting tongue?
We pivot about a buoy, clove hitch a jib pole
and wedge it in the foredeck corner. On a broad reach
for home we break out first beers and then smiles.

Under the jib there's the pilgrimage of hookers
ahead in red winged flight before the wind.
Being last is at least being part of an old line
that rounded the island oratory on MacDara's Day.

A Shoaling at Toombeola Bridge

They came marauding up with the tide
under the bridge between salt and freshwater
gathering themselves in the greatness of their condition,

remembering this shadowed place, this taste,
those far skylarks, this dark entry to the birth place,
the old underworld to be their gravelled graves.

Between peat banks their decompression chamber
is a river risen by recent rains in the big Bens
where they wimple their fins on the water surface

in silver flashes of strength for the falls ahead.
Fat from the sea, beyond feeding now, feeling
that thrust upstream that powered them past

the nets in the neck of the bay and around foul
plugs from the pipes of white shoreline homes
towards the leaks and overflows of small farms

they must outrun and hopeful rods tempting
with the flick of a handmade fly, now they shoal
at dusk under the fading furnace of the west.

Flightless

Where is the heart of the wilderness?
Where is the wilderness of the heart?

Is it here among the marram grass
sitting in the dunes at Sandwood Bay

watching snails after rain, slowly heaving
their heavy shells along grass stems?

Or is it the way people walk across
the sands, slowly, talking little,

taking something into themselves:
the bright light on flat water;

the misted rain, again, drifting
across the far yellow strand;

a white patch on the sea under
that single bubble of white cloud?

These are signs of a pulse
in the wilderness of the heart,

not the arteries of connection
to the heart of the wilderness.

Here John Muir would hear
the way the sound of sand,

sucked back through the teeth
of the tide, leads to the moon.

To find the wilderness of the heart
is to ask the urgent questions: Why

the sun's so strong now, the winters
so wet now? Why the rivers are rising?

Why low islands will shrink
like the skylark's song,

like the oyster beds, like corncrake and cod?
Why it's not so simple as orchids

rising radiant from the bog of decay,
or the beach dead feeding flies in the sun?

At the very heart of the wilderness
there would be no wilderness of the heart,

no journey, no visions, no questions.
Hearts would pump as one, like tides.